THIS
CANDLEWICK BOOK
BELONGS TO:

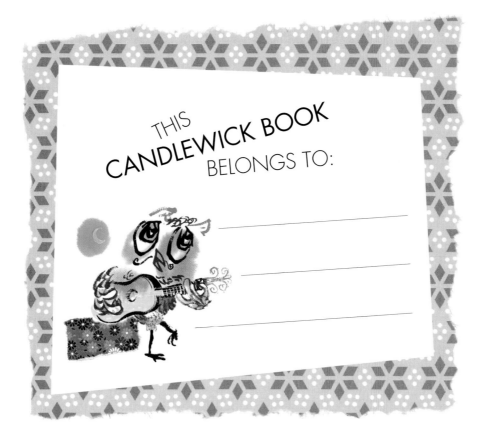

_____

_____

_____

Poems to Speak, Sing, and Shout

A FOOT IN THE MOUTH

selected by

PAUL B. JANECZKO

illustrated by

CHRIS RASCHKA

Candlewick Press

This collection copyright © 2009 by Paul B. Janeczko
Illustrations copyright © 2009 by Chris Raschka
Text copyright © by individual authors as noted in the Acknowledgments, which appear on pages 60–61

First paperback edition 2012

Library of Congress Cataloging-in-Publication Data is available.
Library of Congress Catalog Card Number 2008935581
ISBN 978-0-7636-0663-3 (hardcover)
ISBN 978-0-7636-6083-3 (paperback)

12 13 14 15 16 17 SCP 10 9 8 7 6 5 4 3 2 1
Printed in Humen, Dongguan, China

This book was typeset in Myriad.
The illustrations were done in watercolor, ink, and torn paper.

Candlewick Press
99 Dover Street
Somerville, Massachusetts 02144

visit us at www.candlewick.com

For Mary Lou Watkins,
freeway savant, friend, and SoCal angel
&
in memory of John Skapura (1971–2004)
P. B. J.

For my mother
C. R.

Contents

Introduction

Poetry is sound. Oh sure, it's other things, too, but sound needs to be near the top of the list. To hear the sound of a poem, really hear it, you need to read it out loud. Or have someone read it to you.

All the poems in this book have been chosen because they are terrific candidates for reading aloud. They might be as easy as the six-word "Gigl" by Arnold Spilka, or as "frabjous" and "brillig" as Lewis Carroll's "Jabberwocky," full of delicious nonsense words to roll across your tongue. Many of the poems have very strong rhyme schemes — the poet is showing you how to read the poem through the use of rhyme.

Once you've had some practice reading aloud, you might consider memorizing a poem. A funny limerick, like Edward Lear's "There Was an Old Man in a Barge," could be a good place to start. Memorizing is good for your brain, and it certainly will impress your parents and teachers if you start quoting Walt Whitman's "I Hear America Singing." Students in Ancient

Rome and Greece learned by memorizing, so think of yourself as part of a three-thousand-year-old tradition, a modern-day Homer in the making. And I don't mean Simpson.

You don't have to go it alone, either. Grab a friend and recite Janet S. Wong's "Speak Up," a poem for two voices, or practice your Spanish with Sandra Cisneros's "Good Hot Dogs" and its translation. One person can read the English, and another the Spanish — and then you can switch. Which version is easier? Which pleases you most?

You don't need to be an expert, and if you're not sure how a certain part should sound, ask a parent or teacher. Practice a few times. In no time at all, you'll be able to share the music of a good poem read aloud. If you've never read a poem to somebody, you don't know what you're missing. This book will give you a chance to change that. These three dozen poems are especially satisfying spoken, recited — or shouted! — out loud, from lively rhymes to tricky tongue twisters. Give it a try.

Paul B. Janeczko

The Poems I Like Best

Tracie Vaughn Zimmer

The poems I like best
wear classic black
with vintage accessories
and smell like a new book,
the spine just cracked.

The chitchat overheard on a city bus
or nonsense
volleyed between toddlers
on swings at the park.

My favorite poems
squeeze your hand
on a crowded street and say:
Look.

The poems I like best
wear blue jeans
and smell
like the tack room of a barn:
worn leather and horse.

The varied verses
of a mockingbird's tune
or syllables between brothers
scratching scruffy chins
under the hood of a truck.

My favorite poems
hold a wooden spoon of words
and whisper:
Taste.

Where It Began

Charles R. Smith Jr.

Bouncing brown leather
as a brown baby boy
I remember when Daddy
gave me
my first toy.
A ball
that I bounced
and bounced
some more,
together we bounced
and danced on the floor.

This oversize ball
bigger than me,
I remember bouncing
since the age of three.
Just me and my ball
dancing 'til dark,
when Mama would call me
home from the park.
I remember those times
I remember them well
these thoughts I remember
whenever I dwell
on memories of Dad,
now taken away,

from me
in life
as I talk to and play
with my young son
each and every day
and recite the same words
my dad used to say
like "Play with the team
and always play hard.
Be confident
and never
let down your guard."

Lessons in life
taught with jump shots,
were lifelong lessons
I never forgot.
I'll never forget
cause I'll always remember
the lessons Dad taught
to make me a winner.

WOW!

Favorite

George Ella Lyon

I had an olive drab corduroy coat
A wide-wale corduroy coat
And the grooves went round and round
Instead of up and down
On my olive drab corduroy coat.

Perpendiculars look better on plump girls.
Yeah, perpendiculars look better on plump girls.
But that demon taste is taste
Whatever size your waist.
I loved my wide-wale corduroy coat.

Its barrel buttons slid through olive loops.
I say, its wooden buttons latched by olive loops.
Every time I wore it
I couldn't help but adore it,
My high school corduroy coat.

Its collar was a deep green plush.
Its cuffs, too — deliciously lush.
I may have looked funny
But I called myself Honey
In my olive drab
    Horizontal
       Wide-wale
          Barrel-buttoned
            Plush-collared
              Corduroy
                Coat.

Lone Dog

Irene McLeod

I'm a lean dog, a keen dog, a wild dog and lone,
I'm a rough dog, a tough dog, hunting on my own!
I'm a bad dog, a mad dog, teasing silly sheep;
I love to sit and bay the moon and keep fat souls from sleep.

I'll never be a lap dog, licking dirty feet,
A sleek dog, a meek dog, cringing for my meat.
Not for me the fireside, the well-filled plate.
But shut door and sharp stone and cuff and kick and hate.

Not for me the other dogs, running by my side,
Some have run a short while, but none of them would bide.
O mine is still the lone trail, the hard trail, the best,
Wide wind and wild stars and the hunger of the quest.

17

Jabberwocky

Lewis Carroll

'Twas brillig, and the slithy toves
Did gyre and gimble in the wabe:
All mimsy were the borogoves,
And the mome raths outgrabe.

"Beware the Jabberwock, my son!
The jaws that bite, the claws that catch!
Beware the Jubjub bird, and shun
The frumious Bandersnatch!"

He took his vorpal sword in hand:
Long time the manxome foe he sought —
So rested he by the Tumtum tree,
And stood awhile in thought.

And, as in uffish thought he stood,
The Jabberwock, with eyes of flame,
Came whiffling through the tulgey wood,
And burbled as it came!

One, two! One, two! And through and through
The vorpal blade went snicker-snack!
He left it dead, and with its head
He went galumphing back.

"And hast thou slain the Jabberwock?
Come to my arm, my beamish boy!
O frabjous day! Callooh! Callay!"
He chortled in his joy.

'Twas brillig, and the slithy toves
Did gyre and gimble in the wabe:
All mimsy were the borogoves,
And the mome rats outgrabe.

The Loch Ness Monster's Song

Edwin Morgan

Sssnnnwhuffffll?

Hnwhuffl hhnnwfl hnfl hfl?

Gdroblboblhobngbl gbl gl g g g g glbgl.

Drublhaflablhaflubhafgabhaflhafl fl fl —

gm grawwwww grf grawf awfgm graw gm.

Hovoplodok-doplodovok-plovodokot-doplodokosh?

Splgraw fok fok splgrafhatchgabrlgabrl fok splfok!

Zgra kra gka fok!

Grof grawff gahf?

Gombl mbl bl —

blm plm,

blm plm,

blm plm,

blp.

An Orthographic Lament

Charles Follen Adams

If an S and an I and an O and a U
with an X at the end
spells Sioux,
    And an E and a Y and an E spells eye —
Pray what is a speller to do?
    If an S and an I and a G
and an H and an E and a D
spells sighed,
    Pray what is there left for a speller to do but —
To go and commit Sioux-eye-sighed?

Pasta Parade

Bobbi Katz

Ziti marching in a row —

then capelli d'angelo —

ravioli —

tortellini —

wide lasagna —

slim linguine —

itty bits of pert pastina —

piles of penne mezzanine —

ditali and ditalini —

teeny, weeny tubettini —

farfalle —

and capellini —

nests of woven fettuccine —

　　　Basta!

That's enough already,

Fill my bowl up with spaghetti!

And while you're at it, will you please

pass along the grated cheese.

Corinna

David McCord

Dinner!

Where's Corinna?

Dinner!

Where's Corinner?

Where's Corinner? Innerout?

Corinner risout, no doubt.

Corinner! *Dinner!*

Hearer shout?

And now Corinner resin

from wherever Corinner rasbin.

Corinner reatser dinner

at last — and fast:

most of it sinner.

The Pickety Fence

David McCord

The pickety fence

The pickety fence

Give it a lick it's

The pickety fence

Give it a lick it's

A clickety fence

Give it a lick it's

A lickety fence

Give it a lick

Give it a lick

Give it a lick

With a rickety stick

Pickety

Pickety

Pickety

Pick

Speak Up

Janet S. Wong

You're Korean, aren't you?

Yes.

Why don't you speak
Korean?

Just don't, I guess.

Say something Korean.

I don't speak it.
I can't.

C'mon. Say something.

Halmoni. Grandmother.
Haraboji. Grandfather.
Imo. Aunt.

Say some other stuff.
Sounds funny.
Sounds strange.

Hey, let's listen to you
for a change.

Listen to me?

Say some foreign words.

But I'm American,
can't you see?

Your family came from
somewhere else.
Sometime.

But I was born here.

So was I.

25

I Am Standing —
Girl on Land, Boy at Sea

April Halprin Wayland and
Bruce Balan

Girl on Land	*Boy at Sea*
I am standing	I am standing
feet apart	feet apart
hands on hips	hands on hips
bare feet	bare feet
in damp grass	
	on wood deck
rooted, rooted	
to the earth	moving, moving
	with the waves
I am	I am
climbing	
	climbing
up this	up this
tree	
	mast
swaying	
	swaying
with the wind	with the wind
to and fro	
	to and fro
sparrows, jays, and crows,	
	pelicans, gulls, terns,
and blossoms all around	
	and white caps all around
climbing	
	climbing
up this tree	
	up this mast
in our yard	
	on our boat
in this town	
	in this sea
in my world.	in my world.

27

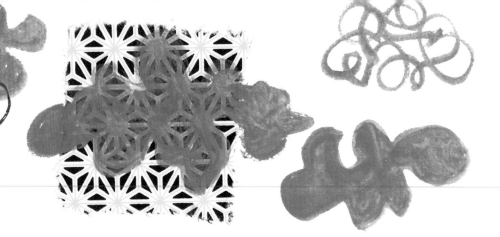

The Sun and the Marigold Talk to Each Other

Patricia Hubbell

"Marigold,

with petals gold,

tell me what you see . . .

Marigold,

with eye of gold,

look up and talk to me . . ."

"Shine down on me

and I will talk . . .

I'll tell you all I see . . .

My roots see blackness,

thick and rich,

my stem sees shades of green—

But O! My eye

sees in the sky

a Marigold—like Me!"

Squirrel and Acorn

Beverly McLoughland

Where's that nut
I hid in the fall?
Bad news!
Bad news!
Can't recall.
Must think,
Try hard,
Somewhere
In the yard.
Look here,
Look there,
Bad news!
Nowhere!

I'm here
Below,
Just under the
Snow,
Off to his
Right —
Well out of
Sight.
He can't
Recall?
Then I'll
Grow tall.
Could be a
Tree.
Good news!
Good news!
Good news
For me!

31

Fishes

Poem for Two Voices

Georgia Heard

Atlantic blue tang		Our	Our
	Zebra pipe	fins	fins
Royal gramma		steer	
	French angel	us	
Cuban hock			like
	Golden butterfly		wings
We	We	We	We
are	are	are	are
fishes	fishes	fishes	fishes
We	We	We	We
shimmer	swim	shimmer	swim
under			
	water		
Our	Our		
mouths	mouths		
open			
and			
	close		
Our	Our		
gills	gills		
sift			
air			
	from		
	water		

A Tomcat Is

J. Patrick Lewis

Night watchman of corners
Caretaker of naps
Leg-wrestler of pillows
Depresser of laps.

A master at whining
And dining on mouse
Afraid of the shadows
That hide in the house.

The bird-watching bandit
On needle-point claws
The chief of detectives
On marshmallow paws.

A crafty yarn-spinner
A stringer high-strung
A buttermilk mustache
A sandpaper tongue.

The dude in the alley
The duke on the couch
Affectionate fellow
Occasional grouch.

Home Poem
Or, the Sad Dog Song

J. Patrick Lewis

Home of the fly: pie.

Home of the frog: log.

Home of the bear: lair.

Home of the gnu: zoo.

Home of the bee: tree.

Home of the mole: hole.

Home of the ants: pants.

Home of the moth: cloth.

Home of the snail: trail.

Home of the otter: water.

Home of the shark: dark.

Home of the snake: lake.

Home of the moose: spruce.

Home of the flea: me!

Macbeth, Act IV, Scene 1

William Shakespeare

Thunder.

Enter the three Witches.

FIRST WITCH

Thrice the brinded cat hath mewed.

SECOND WITCH

Thrice, and once the hedge-pig whined.

THIRD WITCH

Harpier cries "Tis time, 'tis time!'

FIRST WITCH

Round about the cauldron go,

In the poisoned entrails throw.

Toad that under cold stone

Days and nights has thirty-one

Sweltered venom sleeping got,

Boil thou first i' th' charmèd pot.

ALL

Double, double, toil and trouble,

Fire burn, and cauldron bubble.

SECOND WITCH

Fillet of a fenny snake,

In the cauldron boil and bake;

Eye of newt and toe of frog,

Wool of bat and tongue of dog,

Adder's fork and blind-worm's sting,

Lizard's leg and owlet's wing,

For a charm of powerful trouble,

Like a hell-broth boil and bubble.

ALL

Double, double, toil and trouble,

Fire burn, and cauldron bubble.

THIRD WITCH

Scale of dragon, tooth of wolf,

Witches' mummy, maw and gulf

Of the ravined salt-sea shark,

Root of hemlock digged i' th' dark,

Liver of blaspheming Jew,

Gall of goat, and slips of yew

Slivered in the moon's eclipse,

Nose of Turk, and Tartar's lips,

Finger of birth-strangled babe

Ditch-delivered by a drab,

Make the gruel thick and slab.

Add thereto a tiger's chaudron

For th' ingredience of our cauldron.

ALL

Double, double, toil and trouble,

Fire burn, and cauldron bubble.

SECOND WITCH

Cool it with a baboon's blood,

Then the charm is firm and good.

The Owl and the Pussy-Cat

Edward Lear

The Owl and the Pussy-cat went to sea
  In a beautiful pea-green boat,
They took some honey, and plenty of money,
  Wrapped up in a five-pound note.
The Owl looked up to the stars above,
  And sang to a small guitar,
"O lovely Pussy! O Pussy, my love,
  What a beautiful Pussy you are,
    You are,
    You are!
  What a beautiful Pussy you are!"

Pussy said to the Owl, "You elegant fowl!
  How charmingly sweet you sing!
O let us be married! too long we have tarried:
  But what shall we do for a ring?"

They sailed away, for a year and a day,
  To the land where the Bong-Tree grows,
And there in a wood a Piggy-wig stood,
  With a ring at the end of his nose,
    His nose,
    His nose,
  With a ring at the end of his nose.

"Dear Pig, are you willing to sell for one shilling
  Your ring?" Said the Piggy, "I will."
So they took it away, and were married next day
  By the Turkey who lives on the hill.
They dined on mince, and slices of quince,
  Which they ate with a runcible spoon;
And hand in hand, on the edge of the sand,
  They danced by the light of the moon,
    The moon,
    The moon,
  They danced by the light of the moon.

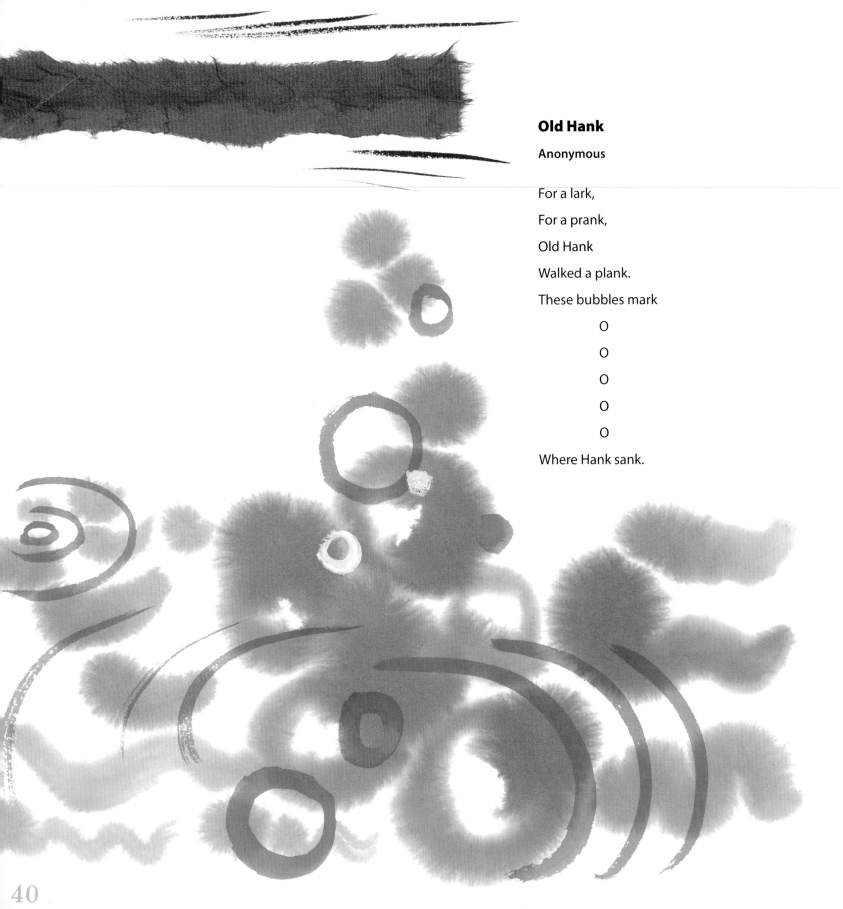

Old Hank

Anonymous

For a lark,

For a prank,

Old Hank

Walked a plank.

These bubbles mark

     O

     O

     O

     O

     O

Where Hank sank.

Gigl

Arnold Spilka

a pigl
wigl
if
u
tigl

Pussycat, Pussycat

Max Fatchen

Pussycat, pussycat, where have you been,

Licking your lips with your whiskers so clean?

Pussycat, pussycat, purring and pudgy,

Pussycat, pussycat, WHERE IS OUR BUDGIE?

Innuendo

David McCord

You are French? *Je suis.*
You speak French? *Mais oui.*
I don't speak French. *Non?*
I speak English. *Bon!*

43

Good Hot Dogs

Sandra Cisneros

for Kiki

Fifty cents apiece
To eat our lunch
We'd run
Straight from school
Instead of home
Two blocks
Then the store
That smelled like steam
You ordered
Because you had the money
Two hot dogs and two pops for here
Everything on the hot dogs
Except pickle lily
Dash those hot dogs
Into buns and splash on
All that good stuff
Yellow mustard and onions
And french fries piled on top all
Rolled up in a piece of wax
Paper for us to hold hot
In our hands
Quarters on the counter
Sit down
Good hot dogs
We'd eat
Fast till there was nothing left
But salt and poppy seeds even
The little burnt tips
Of french fries
We'd eat
You humming
And me swinging my legs

Ricos *Hot Dogs*

translated from the English by Liliana Valenzuela

Cincuenta centavos cada uno

Para almorzar

Corríamos

Directo de la escuela

Sin pasar por la casa

Dos cuadras

Y a la tienda

Que olía a vapor

Tú los pedías

Porque traías el dinero

Dos *hot dogs* y dos sodas

Los *hot dogs* con todo

Menos pepinillos

Pon de volada las salchichas

En los panes y échales

Todo lo rico

Mostaza y cebolla

Y papas fritas encima todo

Envuelto en papel

Encerado para agarrarlo calientito

En las manos

Pesetas en el mostrador

Y a sentarnos

Ricos *hot dogs*

Nos los comíamos

Rápido hasta que no quedaba nada

Más que sal y semillas hasta

Las puntitas quemadas

De las papas

Nos las comíamos

Tú tarareando

Y yo columpiando las piernas

para Kiki

45

My Memories of the Nicaraguan Revolution

Eugenio Alberto Cano Correa

A tear streaming from my eye,

Running through a field seeking refuge,

A road lined with bullet shells instead of pebbles,

An empty wheelbarrow stained red,

A pillar of smoke uniting sky and ground,

A slogan cried from the background,

A hug of protection from my *mamá*.

Mis recuerdos de la revolución nicaragüense

translated from the English by Alexandra López

Una lágrima fluyendo de mi ojo,

Corriendo a campo traviesa buscando refugio,

Un camino marcado por balas servidas en vez de guijarros,

Una carretilla vacía manchada de rojo,

Un pilar de humo uniendo cielo y tierra,

Una consigna gritada desde el fondo,

Un abrazo protector de mi mamá.

One Tooth, Two Tooth, White Tooth, Looth Tooth

Allan Wolf

One tooth. Two teeth.

Baby chew teeth.

Twenty bright teeth.

Pearly white teeth.

Daily use teeth.

Wiggle loose teeth.

Three teeth. Four teeth.

In grow more teeth.

Grown-up new teeth.

Thirty-two teeth.

Not quite right teeth.

Up the Ladder and Down the Wall

Traditional

Up the ladder and down the wall,

Penny an hour will serve us all.

You buy butter and I'll buy flour,

And we'll have a pudding in half an hour.

   With —

        salt,

           mustard,

              vinegar,

                 pepper.

"What's Your Name?"
Traditional

"What's your name?"

"Mary Jane."

"Where do you live?"

"Womber Lane."

"What do you do?"

"Keep a school."

"How many scholars?"

"Twenty-two."

"How many more?"

"Twenty-four."

"What's your number?"

"Cucumber."

WOMBER

There Was a Young Woman from Boise

Douglas Florian

There was a young woman from Boise

Whose sneakers were squeaky and noisy.

    She set them to boil

    In sunflower oil,

Then she jogged all the way to New Joisy.

53

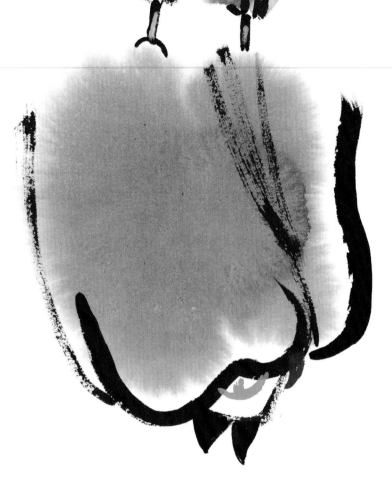

The Nose

J. Patrick Lewis

The bat clings to the ceiling above,

Wrapped in wings like a hand in a glove,

    Too afraid to expose

    To his neighbors a nose

That only a mother could love.

There Was an Old Man in a Barge

Edward Lear

There was an Old Man in a Barge,

Whose Nose was exceedingly large;

But in fishing by night,

It supported a light,

Which helped that Old Man in a Barge.

Come, Drum!

Avis Harley

Come, drum! Sound out the day!
Your humdrum frame has much to tell.
Roll out your rhythms and sweep us away.

Pump out the heartbeat for jazz and ballet:
Kindle the dancers who spin under spell.
Come, drum! Sound out the day!

Pound out the surf; thunder the spray;
Answer the raging, roaring swell.
Roll out your rhythms and sweep us away.

Shake out the song in an old roundelay;
Echo those voices that rose and fell.
Come, drum! Sound out the day!

Crack open night with a fireworks display;
Explode into gold each shimmering shell.
Roll out your rhythms and sweep us away.

Dance in our veins and pulse in our play;
Exult in the language you know so well.
Come, drum! Sound out the day!
Roll out your rhythms and sweep us away.

Where Lizzie Lived

A Haunted Tale

Rebecca Kai Dotlich

The chimney's tumbled down, old doors
pout from hinges, rotted floors
grumble slightly as we're walking.

Do you hear Miss Lizzie talking?

Steps have crumbled, that's not all,
her portrait captivates the hall.
The rocking chair is barely rocking.

Could that be Miss Lizzie knocking?

A spoon inside a china cup
slumbers, as we pick it up
a tinkling sound, so slight of tapping.

Shhh, Miss Lizzie might be napping.

Wind chimes stir, and from a hook
abides an iron bell, a book
lies open at the window, sighing.

Or is it only Lizzie crying?

57

I Hear America Singing

Walt Whitman

I hear America singing, the varied carols I hear;

Those of mechanics — each one singing his, as it should

be, blithe and strong;

The carpenter singing his, as he measures his plank or

beam,

The mason singing his, as he makes ready for work, or

leaves off work;

The boatman singing what belongs to him in his boat —

the deck-hand singing on the steamboat deck;

The shoemaker singing as he sits on his bench —

the hatter singing as he stands;

The wood-cutter's song — the ploughboy's, on his way in

the morning, or at noon intermission, or at

sundown;

The delicious singing of the mother, or of the young

wife at work — or of the girl sewing or washing —

Each singing what belongs to him or her, and to none

else;

The day what belongs to the day — At night the party

of young fellows, robust, friendly,

Singing, with open mouths, their strong melodious

songs.

Acknowledgments

"The Poems I Like Best" by Tracie Vaughn Zimmer, from *42 Miles* by Tracie Vaughn Zimmer. Copyright © 2008 by Tracie Vaughn Zimmer. Reprinted by permission of Clarion Books, an imprint of Houghton Mifflin Harcourt Publishing Company.

"Where It Began" by Charles R. Smith Jr. Copyright © 2009 by Charles R. Smith Jr. Used by permission of the author.

"Favorite" by George Ella Lyon. Copyright © 2009 by George Ella Lyon. Reprinted by permission of the author.

"The Loch Ness Monster's Song" by Edwin Morgan, from *Poems of Thirty Years* by Edwin Morgan. Copyright © by Carcanet Press Ltd. Reprinted by permission of Carcanet Press Ltd.

"Pasta Parade" by Bobbi Katz. Copyright © 1996 by Bobbi Katz. Reprinted by permission of the author.

"Corinna" by David McCord, from *One at a Time* by David McCord. Copyright © 1965, 1966 by David McCord. Reprinted by permission of Little, Brown and Company.

"The Pickety Fence" by David McCord, from *One at a Time* by David McCord. Copyright © 1965, 1966 by David McCord. Reprinted by permission of Little, Brown and Company.

"Speak Up" by Janet S. Wong, from *Good Luck Gold and Other Poems* by Janet S. Wong. Copyright © 1994 by Janet S. Wong. Reprinted by permission of Margaret K. McElderry, an imprint of Simon & Schuster Children's Publishing Division.

"I Am Standing" by April Halprin Wayland and Bruce Balan. Copyright © 2007 by Bruce Balan and April Halprin Wayland. Reprinted by permission of the authors.

"The Sun and the Marigold Talk to Each Other" by Patricia Hubbell, from *Black Earth, Gold Sun* by Patricia Hubbell. Copyright © 2001 by Patricia Hubbell. Reprinted by permission of Marian Reiner for the author.

"Ping-Pong Poem" by Douglas Florian, from *Bing Bang Boing*. Copyright © 1994 by Douglas Florian. Reprinted by permission of Harcourt, Inc.

"Us Two" by A. A. Milne, from *Now We Are Six* by A. A. Milne, illustrated by E. H. Shepard. Copyright 1927 by E. P. Dutton, © renewed 1955 by A. A. Milne. Reprinted by permission of Dutton Children's Books, a division of Penguin Young Readers Group, a member of Penguin Group (USA) Inc., New York, and Egmont UK Ltd., London. All rights reserved.

"Squirrel and Acorn" by Beverly McLoughland, first published in *Spider* magazine, 1998. Copyright © 1998 by Beverly McLoughland. Reprinted by permission of the author.

"Fishes: Poem for Two Voices" by Georgia Heard, from *Creatures of Earth, Sea, and Sky* by Georgia Heard, published by Boyds Mills Press. Copyright © 1992 by Georgia Heard. Reprinted by permission of Curtis Brown Ltd.

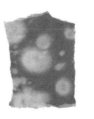

PAUL B. JANECZKO is a poet and teacher and has edited more than twenty award-winning poetry anthologies for young people. He has collaborated with illustrator Chris Raschka on two previous anthologies, *A Poke in the I* and *A Kick in the Head*. Both books were American Library Association Notable Children's Books and *School Library Journal* Best Books of the Year. *A Poke in the I* was also a Bank Street College Best Children's Book of the Year, and *A Kick in the Head* was a Claudia Lewis Award Winner. Paul B. Janeczko lives in Hebron, Maine, with his wife and daughter.

CHRIS RASCHKA is the illustrator of more than twenty highly praised books for children, including the Caldecott Medal–winning *The Hello, Goodbye Window;* the Caldecott Honor Book *Yo! Yes?; A Primer About the Flag; I Pledge Allegiance; A Child's Christmas in Wales;* and *The Grasshopper's Song: An Aesop's Fable Revisited.* He also illustrated *A Poke in the I* and *A Kick in the Head,* both edited by Paul B. Janeczko. Chris Raschka lives in New York City with his wife and son.